In all but the poorest countries of the world, most of the people now alive will live to be old. This is a new situation. Only a hundred years ago, it was unusual for someone to live to 70 or 80 years of age. Now most families have at least one relative who has lived longer than the Bible's "Three score years and ten" (70). Because this is a new situation for us, we don't really know how to treat older people. We tend to imagine that someone who is old is in some way different from the rest of us and will have different feelings and needs. But growing older is not just something that happens to you at the end of your life. Ageing is a life-long process, and its effects are so gradual that very few people ever feel "old".

Most of us have a mental image of what old people are like and how they behave. The words that are used are fairly depressing – wrinkled, boring, frail, lonely, living in the past. But really, older people don't match these stereotypes. People over 70 differ from each other as much as younger people. One elderly woman chooses to live very quietly. She has never been a sociable person; her interests and hobbies are all concerned with her home, just as they have always been. Her neighbour of the same age is outgoing, takes a lively interest in current issues, and enjoys a good laugh with her friends.

We remain individuals whatever our age. Look at the "old" man or woman on the bus with you. Now think of them in their twenties: think of everything they have been through in their lives, and what younger people can learn from their very varied experiences.

In some countries where there is no "safety net" of welfare services, old people rely on their families for care and support.

CHAPTER 1

OUR AGEING WORLD

> Women outnumber men in all the older age-groups, particularly among the very oldest where there are four or five times as many women as men.

In this century, the population of the world has grown faster than ever before. Immunisation programmes, discoveries of new medicines and improvements in preventative health care have meant that more and more children survive into adult hood, even in the poorest countries in the world. Today, we are seeing that people are not only surviving to reach adulthood, but that more and more of them are living into old age. By the year 2100 there will be two and a half billion people – a quarter of all the world's population – over the age of 60. Most of these older people will be women, who have a life expectancy on average five years greater than that of men.

A greying world
In Europe and North America older people represent 14 per cent of the total population. This situation has been arrived at fairly slowly, with the growth of industry and city living during the past century and a half. The increase in the percentage of over-60s in the population will continue in these countries, but the really rapid changes will happen in the developing world. In Africa, Asia and Latin America, the number of elderly people will almost double within the next 20 years.

These changes will affect the way of life of people all over the world. How will we, and the generations to come, deal with the problems raised by this ageing of our population? How can we make sure that growing old will not mean poverty and dependence? How can older people be helped to look after themselves more effectively? Can families be strengthened so that they can care for

their old more easily? Who will look after those who become frail and infirm?

Retirement – a new invention

A hundred years ago, practically no one retired. Men and women carried on working as they had always done until they were too sick and frail to continue. Today, almost everyone who is in paid employment eventually retires. The age of retirement is usually between 60 and 70, with the trend being towards retirement at an ever earlier age.

Men and women giving up paid work today are not in any sense "old". They can look forward to another 20 or even 30 years of life and are mostly fit and active. For many newly retired people,

Retirement need not mean a sedentary life – many older people take up new interests and hobbies.

leaving work is not something they want to do but is forced upon them by regulations about retirement age. Others look forward to giving up a job that has become a tiresome burden. But whatever their feelings about retirement, it is, for most people, one of the important milestones in their lives: like starting work, getting married or having a child.

> "I dreaded retirement. My friends were all colleagues at work and I hardly knew anyone else. I didn't know how I was going to fill the days." John, aged 62

Mid-life adjustment
In the past, retirement was mainly a problem faced by men. Now that more women work outside the home, they too can experience the loss of their working identity. For those women whose work was caring for their children an adjustment has to come even earlier. With the trend towards smaller families, women in their forties have faced an "empty nest", with their children having grown and left home.

For many couples there are problems of adjustment. For example if the man has thought of himself as the "provider", his partner will need to support him through feelings of uselessness.

One of the tasks which often falls on newly retired people is the care of their own, very elderly parents. A man or woman in her sixties is likely to be the sole support of a parent, usually the mother, in her eighties or nineties. (In the over-80 age group, women outnumber men in a ratio of 4:1.)

Residential care or care in the community?

Many people believe that most very old people live in residential or nursing homes. But this is not true. In Britain, for example, only three per cent of the elderly population live in a residential home or hospital, and even in the Netherlands, which has the highest proportion of people in homes in the world, only nine per cent of the elderly population are in care.

This means that in the richer countries of the world, more than 90 per cent of the elderly population are living in private households, either alone or with relatives. Yet as people grow older, they need more support and care. They are more likely to have an illness requiring treatment in hospital. Older hospital patients are also more likely to need to stay longer. As the population grows older, the expense of providing health and

With the help of other people in the community, many more old people can remain in their own home.

social care increases. Also, it is the numbers of the very old, those over 75, which are increasing fastest; and it is the very old who make the greatest demand on public health and social services.

Estimates of the percentage of different age-groups within the population over 65 in Britain.

	1980	1990	2000	2020	2040
65-69	33.9	32.5	29.9	31.0	25.4
70-79	48.2	46.2	47.9	48.8	49.7
80+	17.8	21.2	22.1	20.1	24.8

OECD 1988

Time to give
It is easy to fall into the trap of seeing the ageing of our world as solely a problem. Yet many men and women are entering later life fitter and more able to look after themselves and others than ever before. Many older people retire only to throw themselves into unpaid activities which benefit their communities, charities or pressure groups. Many others, particularly women, do not involve themselves much in the wider community, but play an essential part in providing care to older and younger relatives, friends and neighbours.

"My granddaughter leaves her little boy with me in the mornings when she goes to work. It's only part-time, but at two years old he's quite a handful!" Joan, aged 63

For a son or daughter caring for an old parent, there can be a loving satisfaction in looking after the person who once looked after you. For the parent too, the situation can arouse strong emotions. It can be harder to surrender authority, to admit that you can no longer cope and that your own child, now grown, must be responsible for you from now on.

Most families would prefer to care for their relatives at home, but sometimes families and job commitments make it impossible.

CHAPTER 2

WHO LOOKS AFTER WHOM, WORLD-WIDE?

Four- and even five-generation families are not unheard of today. Many people become grandparents in their forties and it is not unusual for great-grandparents to take an active part in child-care.

Older people often talk of the changes in family life which they have seen. They refer to a situation where families were closer and larger, and will often suggest that family ties have weakened as we have grown richer and have greater freedom to choose different ways of life. It is true that there have been great changes in family structures in the rich, developed countries. Large families, once the norm, are now rare. The extended family – where three or more generations live together – has almost disappeared in the West, and as the number of single parent families has increased, even the nuclear family – mum, dad and their children – is giving way to new living patterns. Western societies seem to be breaking into smaller and smaller units. In Europe 80 per cent of elderly couples live separately from their families. Half of all women above retirement age live alone, more than double the figure 40 years ago.

But even though those who talk of a changed family life are accurate, there are still millions of old people in the Western world who are supported and cared for by their relatives – usually by their female relatives. In Britain, for example, there are more than a million people providing full-time care at home to a dependent relative. Despite the help they receive from community nurses, home helps, health visitors and good neighbours, by far the greatest burden of care falls on these relatives.

Older people in the developing world
Caring families in the developed countries can expect at least some support from the state. There

are pensions, allowances, and health and social workers, and even if this support is often inadequate, at a time of crisis the old person can go into hospital or to a residential or nursing home. In the developing countries, the situation is quite different. Most governments have very little health provision and caring for the old and sick is left largely to families and voluntary organisations. The plight of frail, old people can then be much worse, because families are not able to provide this care. Children have moved to the cities to find work and this, together with a trend towards smaller families, is contributing to the break up of extended families. Older people in country areas are often left alone, or follow their children to towns only to find themselves living alone, in a shanty town, with no help available. Without a safety net of health and social care, these old people face total destitution.

A range of lifestyles
North America has pioneered the retirement community – whole residential areas inhabited entirely by elderly people. For the people who live in them they offer security, a wide range of social and recreational activities and a life-style devoted entirely to leisure. It is easy to criticise these communities, to call them unnatural because there are no children or young adults, but it is obvious that they are extremely popular with residents and that, for many people, they offer a sociable setting in which to spend the rest of their lives.

The retirement community has not yet developed to any great extent in Europe, although it seems likely to do so. The countries of Northern Europe are showing an interest in housing developments in the South – particularly in Spain. Richer pensioners from Germany, the Scandinavian countries and from Britain are moving to the warmer countries of the South, either for the winter or to live permanently in a warmer climate. It remains to be seen what impact the presence of this group of comparatively richer old people will have upon the economy and way of life of the Southern European countries, particularly as the newcomers grow older and need more health care.

Residential homes vary. The best offer stimulation and companionship as well as physical care.

Less drastic than moving to another country is a move to another town or to a smaller, easier to run, home in the same neighbourhood. In Britain, for

example, many retired couples choose to move to the seaside towns of Wales and Northern England or to the South coast. Some towns and countries in the South have retired populations of more than 40 per cent, placing great burdens on local health and social services. People may also choose to move into sheltered accommodation, either privately owned or run by a local authority. These are small flats (often there is only one bedroom) and there is a warden available who checks regularly that all is well.

> "I have a call button, so that I could get help at once, if I needed it." Mrs D, aged 76

Needing extra care
Most older people spend their lives independently in their own homes, although many eventually die in hospital after a final illness. There are, however, a minority who choose to enter a residential or nursing home, when the struggle to cope independently becomes too great.

Residential homes may be run privately as businesses, by voluntary organisations on a not-for-profit basis, or by the local authority.

> "They're all very kind. I couldn't ask for better care. I've gained some things and lost some things by coming here. On the one hand, I feel secure and free from worry. I can have help when I need it and plenty of company. On the other hand I really miss my independence and privacy, and my own home with its memories and familiar things." Mr Williams, aged 86

Some retirement communities pioneered in the United States offer many recreational activities. But these communities tend to be more for the active and fit elderley.

Younger relatives or friends and neighbours may encourage an older person to go into residential care. Families worry about the risks if a frail old person is living alone. They may also be worn out by the effort of trying to help a relative cope, perhaps visiting several times a day to help with washing, dressing and meal preparation. The ideal for those who provide residential care is to give residents choice about their way of life. Unfortunately, real choice is difficult to provide and coming into care often means giving up the right to make decisions about your daily life.

**"I'm glad I get help to look after my mum"
Phyllis, aged 68**

Village life in the developing world

The kind of decision that a pensioner living in Copenhagen might make, to move to live in a retirement housing development in Spain, is unimaginable to someone the same age living in a rural village in Bangladesh or Peru. For the majority of older people in the rural areas of the developing world, their lifestyle is no different to that of the rest of the community. If there is poverty, it is a shared poverty. Older people expect to work all their lives. They also take it for granted that their grown children will care for them in their old age. Unlike retired people in developed countries, villagers in Asia or Africa will have no pension at all, or else a very tiny one.

In traditional societies, men and women go on working until they are too frail to continue. A fixed age for retirement is still unusual.

The care provided by voluntary agencies in poor countries varies a great deal. In some cases it is extremely basic and the residents of a home may have no more than a bed-space in a crowded dormitory. In other cases the residents' living conditions may be much more affluent than those of the ordinary people in the community surrounding the home. Such a situation can provoke questions. Is it right to provide very high standards of care and accommodation for just a few individuals, in the midst of surrounding poverty? On the other hand, should you deliberately choose *not* to provide the best quality of care that you can? This dilemma is particularly acute for charities working among the poorest villages in the developing world.

> **"The residents of our home had literally nothing. They had been forced to beg for a little food and had nowhere to sleep except the street." Social worker, 1989**

The only real solutions to this problem may lie in the development of whole communities so that they can afford to care for their old people and provide economic security for those without families. But the old people in greatest need cannot afford to wait for an improvement in general living standards. They lack the basic requirements of life – food, clothing and shelter. Religious and other voluntary agencies are often the sole support of such destitute old people.

CASE STUDY

Jack and Sylvia recently celebrated their 40th wedding anniversary. Surrounded by family and friends, they seemed to be the ideal older couple. But when Jack had first retired, things were not going well.

Jack is now 74 and Sylvia is 66. When he retired nine years ago, it meant a big upheaval for them both. Jack's work had been extremely important to him. When he left, the company held a party for him and presented him with a clock. He and Sylvia went for a month on a long-planned trip to New Zealand, to visit their married son. After that, Jack did not really know what to do with himself. He was bored and miserable.

It was not easy for Sylvia either. She had not worked outside the home and she was used to having the house to herself during the week. She did voluntary work at the local hospital, and two afternoons a week she played bridge with friends. "When Jack retired, he was always under my feet," she said. "He didn't like me to go out, but he didn't like it when my friends came round to see me either.

Because he didn't have to get ready for work, he used to sit around in his dressing gown until lunch time."

Sylvia was in the habit of finishing her housework early and having the day free to spend as she liked. She found it hard to be understanding when Jack complained of boredom and feeling useless.

Luckily, before Jack and Sylvia had reached the point of complete breakdown, a welfare worker from his old company recruited him to the firm's retirement club. He is now the membership secretary and has put his skills into the task of expanding the number of ex-employees involved. He has also become active in a local community group. With interests of his own, Jack has become easier to live with and less dependent on Sylvia. Their problems have brought Jack and Sylvia closer.

CHAPTER 3

THE AGEING PROCESS

As families become more mobile and increasing numbers of marriages end in divorce, more and more children grow up without a close relationship with grandparents or great-grandparents.

A human life can be seen as dividing into two parts. The first is the phase of growth and development and the second is the phase of ageing and deterioration. Until about the age of 20, a human is growing and developing. After that, we begin to decline, but the rate of decline is usually very gradual and we can do a great deal to influence this.

John was doing a school project on ageing, and as part of his research he interviewed Dr Brady, a consultant geriatrician, at her office in his local hospital.

"Physical ageing is a life-long process," Dr Brady told him. "It isn't something which occurs suddenly overnight. It happens over a lifetime, and will affect different people in different ways. But some physical changes are simply a normal part of the ageing process and will happen to everyone who survives for a normal lifespan."

"When I think of an old person, I think of a stooped, white-haired person with wrinkles, peering at a book held right up to their face, or cupping their hand to their ear to catch what you're saying," said John.

"Well, let's take those things one by one," said Dr Brady. "First of all, eyesight. The lens of the eye becomes harder and less elastic, leading to shortsightedness. Older people can also find it harder to distinguish colours.

Then hearing. Many people notice hearing loss by the age of 50. This occurs partly because the tiny bones in the ear, which normally vibrate with sound, fuse together, making it difficult to hear high-pitched sounds. On the other hand, hearing loss may be the result of working in a noisy environment for many years.

Most people have some grey or white hair by their mid-forties, through lost pigment. Their hair may become thinner – many people become bald. Skin loses its elasticity, which is why we get Wrinkles, and skin may also look different because of changes in pigment or damage to tiny veins.

Senses like taste and smell become less acute. Because of a loss of cartilage in the spine, many people become shorter in their seventies and eighties. And because the lungs become less elastic, there is a decrease in lung capacity, which means that old people often get short of breath. Their lungs can't take in as much air as they need, especially when they are doing something like climbing stairs."

"...behind the appearance of age I am the same person with the same thoughts as when I was younger." J B Priestly

Mental changes in old age
What about mental changes?" asked John. "Although intellectual capacity definitely stops growing after our early twenties, this doesn't actually mean that we stop learning. Intellectual capacity is not the same as intellectual achievement or wisdom. These continue to grow, affected by experience, technical skill and personal aptitudes. But for how long? We do know that older people may find it slightly more difficult to acquire new concepts or to use new information quickly and accurately when working under pressure. Short-

term memory may also be affected by ageing, although memory for long-gone events is usually unaffected. For the majority of older people, the normal ageing process makes very little difference to intellectual capacity. The number of brain cells reduces as we grow older, but the many millions that remain ensure that we can continue to function normally. Normal ageing need hold no fears.

But a minority of old people do suffer from some kind of brain failure. This is the condition that we call senility and is now more often described as dementia. This brain failure is, so far, permanent and irreversible and tends to get worse. The most common form of dementia is Alzheimer's disease. This disease is more common among the very old, and may affect as many as one in five of the people over 80. Medical research is being directed towards understanding and possibly finding a cure for dementia; and it is already abundantly clear that brain failure is a disease, and has no part in the normal ageing process of the human being."

As old as you feel

We can do a great deal to affect the rate at which the body's ageing occurs. The first influence on ageing is your general fitness throughout life. Fitness can be measured by the ability of the body to respond to challenge without upset. If running to catch a bus would leave you breathless, with your heart pounding, for ten minutes afterwards, then you're probably pretty unfit. Becoming unfit is part of growing up in our societies. Older people are much less able to cope with immobility than children, but it is the ten year olds who go out and play baseball, whilst their 40 year old parents sit about and drink coffee. Improving your level of fitness can be achieved at any age. Older people lose strength and stamina mainly because they're less active and not because they are older. Exercise around retirement age is especially important for continuing to maintain independence in later life. It can also prevent some illnesses by reducing blood pressure and slowing the rate at which bones become thinner and more likely to break easily. Carefully regulated exercise is also important for people with angina or other heart and chest diseases, although in these cases medical advice is essential before exercising. Exercise classes can also provide social interest.

Whatever your age, you can improve your health by a programme of regular exercise.

The other main influence on ageing is the individual's own attitude.

"One of the good things about being the age I am now is the release from strict routines and timetables. I can choose what I want to do, what to wear, where to go, on any particular day. I'm more free now than I've ever been." May, aged 65, recently retired.

Dressing up in costume and doing something silly can still be fun, even if you are old.

If people face the changes ageing brings with a positive, open attitude then ageing can really mean adding life to years and not just years to life. For many people, retirement from work is the opportunity for new projects.

"If I'd known I was going to live this long I'd have taken better care of myself."
Jazz musician Eubie Blake on his 100th birthday.

Ageism

But it is hard to keep a positive attitude to ageing, if you live in an ageist society, one which discriminates against people on the grounds of age. The people of the developed world are obsessed with youth. Older people are often overlooked or ignored because they are thought "too old" to have a useful contribution to make or a helpful attitude to share. Despite equal opportunity legislation in some countries, older people still find that they are discriminated against when they apply to join clubs, go on courses or take up employment opportunities. There are age limits on insurances, franchises and even holidays.

Our society treats older people very badly. In contrast to many other societies, in which old people are respected and valued for their experience, we often dismiss them as "poor old dears". Often we think of them only as a burden which the rest of us have to carry.

This attitude is expressed in our low level of social support for older people. The state pensions they receive are a poor return for a lifetime of work which has benefited all of us. This may have been work which went towards creating the world we live in – like building our roads and houses – or work which went into caring for and raising the children who in turn became our parents.

Outside the Western countries, the situation

may well be different. One factor which the many diverse cultures of Africa, Asia and Latin America have had in common is the high regard in which the elders of a community were traditionally held. No important decision, whether it was the arrangements for a marriage, the sharing and use of land or the settlement of a dispute was made without first consulting the senior members of the community. In a traditional society, most of the practical knowledge and skills which helped the community to survive were held by elderly people. Sadly, this situation may be changing. New ways of doing things, together with the movement of young people to the cities has meant that the experience of older people is less relevant. Their contribution may be dismissed as unimportant in just the same way as happens in the more affluent societies of the West.

Low self-esteem

Maggie Kuhn, the founder of the Grey Panther movement in the United States, has written and spoken about "grey pride". She encourages older people not to be satisfied with a place in a rocking chair by the fire. Too many old people themselves share the ageist attitudes of our societies. It is not all right to pay old people pensions of less than half the average working wage, to deprive them of dignity and privacy in homes and hospitals, even to take away their names and simply call them "Gran" or "Pop". Yet many old people are treated this way and accept it without making too much of a fuss or a protest. If you have low self-esteem and low expectations, it is only too easy to patronise or

ignore you.

It is not too surprising that many old people accept inferior treatment without protest. Their past lives have often been marked by hardship and they have learned to make the best of what they get. Men and women who struggled all their lives to make ends meet may gratefully accept situations which younger people would react to angrily. People retiring now have had a very different experience and they will expect to continue with an affluent and comfortable way of life in which they play a full part. They object to being described as a "sweet old person". It means they are not being taken seriously.

Mrs Thatcher, the British Prime Minister, is seen as a powerful person, not as a woman of retirement age. Ageism can be set aside when an older person has great political or economic influence.

CHAPTER 4

THE FOURTH AGE

This old woman
is 112 years of
age and she is
one of the oldest
people in the
United States.
She is highly
unusual, although
it is becoming
quite common to
reach an age of 80
or 90.

Retirement, sometimes called the Third Age, can be a time of new opportunities. Active, fit people with new leisure and money to spend enjoying it can move to new communities, take up fresh interests and find great satisfaction in a changed lifestyle. Social gerontologists, who study the lifestyles of older people, draw a distinction between this period of late maturity and old age – the so-called Fourth Age. The description "Fourth Age" is used for the period at the end of a life when a person may need help and support in order to continue to live independently. Human beings vary enormously and some individuals are fit and active at 90 years of age, requiring no help.

"I make a point of walking the mile to the town centre every day". Mr Petersen, aged 87

Others years younger may be frail and housebound. Generally speaking, however, it is the oldest people, those over 75, who are most likely to need medical treatment and help with the activities of daily life. It is this age-group who are also most likely to suffer from the chronic diseases of old age – arthritis, diabetes, heart disease, strokes, cancers and Alzheimer's disease. Today there are 34 million people over the age of 80 in the world; by the year 2020, there will be over a hundred million. Over the next 40 years the developing world will see an increase of nearly 400 per cent in the numbers of very old people. This huge increase of the numbers of very old people, worldwide, presents a major challenge to our societies' capacity to look after their weakest members.

Causes of dependency

A large survey of older people in Britain and the United States, conducted some years ago, asked them what caused them the greatest worry. More than half of the men and women questioned replied that "losing their good health" was their greatest worry.

Even in the richest countries of the world, some old people live in unsatisfactory housing and have to choose between heating and eating.

"So long as I have my health, I can cope with any other problems." Mrs S, aged 72

Since then, other studies have confirmed that health problems are the main difficulty for frail old people, whether they live alone or with their families. There are, of course, other problems which make it hard to achieve an independent, secure old age. Poverty is a problem for many older people and their lives can be made stressful by loneliness and the effort of living in poor housing, perhaps in a neighbourhood where they feel frightened and at risk.

The cost of health care
Caring for the health needs of an elderly population is expensive. In the West, providing geriatric wards, nursing homes, community care, specialised staff and all the other medical services for the old is taking up an ever-increasing share of both public and private funds. In the Netherlands an average of £225 per person per year is spent on health care for those under 20; for those between 65 and 79 the cost of health care is £575. For those over 80, the cost of health care rises to more than £2,000. In the United States, Medicare – the government health scheme for elderly people – spends a quarter of its whole budget treating people during the last year of their lives.

People are now looking for new ways of meeting these demands for care. All over Europe, long stay geriatric wards are being closed and there are moves towards more community-based care systems. Day care, home care assistants and so on are seen as an attractive alternative to residential care. For governments, care in the community has a double attraction. Not only does it offer older people the chance to be supported in their own homes, but it is also a cheaper option!

> "I have long conversations with the people on television. I interrupt and tell them they're talking rubbish. You'd think I was mad if you came in and saw me."
> James, aged 69

If you are still mobile, joining social clubs, doing voluntary work, helping out with friends and neighbours, or taking part in church activities are all possible ways of overcoming isolation. But loneliness remains one of the greatest problems for older people in the developed world.

Increasingly, it is a problem in the developing world too, particularly among old people left behind in the rural areas as younger relatives have migrated to the cities. The worst loneliness, however, is to be found in the relatively affluent societies, where older people have lost the sense of belonging which comes with a clearly defined role in the community.

Grief and loss

No individual, as he or she grows older, escapes the experience of loss and bereavement. To the loss of loved partners, relatives and friends is often added loss of mobility, loss of strength and capacity, loss of an accustomed home and occupation. There are no easy answers to offer to men and women at the end of their lives who are struggling to adjust to grief and loss.

Loneliness and isolation

More than a third of all elderly people – and half of those aged over 80 – live alone. This was the conclusion of the most recent household survey in

Britain. For women, the situation was even more extreme, with almost half of the female population over 65 living alone and 61 per cent of women over 80. Many of these solitary people are very lonely.

Loneliness is often the worst problem endured by old people in towns and cities. To be surrounded by people, none of whom have any interest in you, can cause great misery.

Widowhood is common in the Fourth Age – we have already mentioned that women outnumber men by four to one among the over-80s. This is another situation in which older people in the developed world may actually find adjustment harder than in a more traditional society, because in Northern Europe and in North America many of the old rituals of mourning have been abandoned. Bereaved relatives are expected to pick up the threads of their lives and carry on as before.

> "They were embarrassed when I wanted to talk about him. I felt that they avoided me."
> Mrs F , aged 70

When an old person has had to give up her home and move into residential care, there is also a kind of bereavement. Even when she understands that there was no alternative, there is grief about the loss of independence and familiar surroundings. Again, families and those who work in residential care may not be able to deal with the person's grief and pain. Relatives may feel guilty and will want to reassure her that "it's all for the best", while staff may not have time to sit and talk.

A good death

An experienced physician, specialising in the care of elderly people, has said that one of the aims of medical care of the aged should be:

> "To give old people a good death as well as a good life. We need to be concerned about the quality of life of people with terminal illness. Interference and repeated surgery may not be the best care." Dr H

Very few old people are really afraid of dying, but the physician is referring to something that does cause many older people to be afraid – the thought of being kept alive by mechanical means or suffering from brain failure. The idea of a "living will" has been pioneered in the United States, where a person, earlier in life, states that he or she does not wish to be treated under certain circumstances.

There are complicated ethical issues involved. Euthanasia, sometimes called "mercy killing", is a crime and relatives have been prosecuted for helping a family member to die. Is there a point, however, when those suffering from terminal illnesses should be able to refuse further treatment and choose to die in peace? Should doctors and families be allowed to decide that a dying person should no longer receive intensive care?

This older woman went to America as an immigrant 50 years ago. Now she gains comfort in tending her husband's grave, in the cemetery occupied by her community.

There are also questions for politicians and policy makers. What proportion of public funds should be allocated to caring for the very old and chronically ill? Should we devote expensive technology to extending the lifespan of very old people? Should scarce research funds be allocated to investigating ways of prolonging life, or would it be better to look at how to improve the quality of life, perhaps by researching cures for arthritis rather than organ transplants? All these questions will become even more important as the numbers of the very old increase, all over the world.

Abuse of Old People

In the past few years there has been a growing concern about physical and mental abuse of frail old people. A recent report from the British Geriatrics Society suggested that there are as many as 500,000 elderly people at risk of being abused

This man is reassured by the doctor in hospital. However in the richer countries of the world most people die in hospital, often without the comforting presence of family and friends.

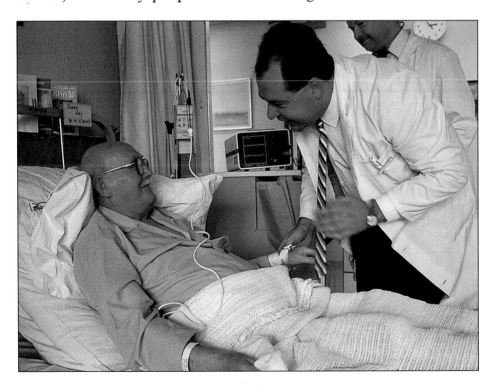

by those who care for them, at home or in residential homes and hospitals.

We don't like to think that helpless old people might be hurt and bullied by their own relatives, but the most likely victim of abuse is in fact a very old woman, usually incontinent and perhaps suffering from dementia, living with an adult child.

"Often the abuse is carried out by ordinary caring men and women, who are at their wits end through tiredness and lack of support." Family doctor, 1989

As more and more men and women survive into the Fourth Age and need to be helped to live independently in the community, this problem is likely to increase. The strain of caring for someone who needs help with feeding, washing and going to the toilet, who may sleep badly and need attention during the night as well as in the day-time, can bring even a loving relative to the point of violence.

Abuse of old people in homes and hospitals is less likely to take the form of physical violence, but there are more subtle forms of abuse. Patients may be over-sedated, to keep them passive and less troublesome. For the same reasons, patients likely to wander or to fall frequently may be tied to chairs or beds, leaving staff free to attend other duties. Such abuse is, thankfully, uncommon. The majority of people who choose to work with the very old are kind and sympathetic. As with child abuse, it seems that we are only now beginning to realise the extent of a previously hidden problem.

CASE STUDY

Stella is 87. She has been a widow for 25 years. She lives alone and her only relative still living in the same inner-city neighbourhood is her grand-daughter, Cathy. Stella has arthritis and has had two hip operations. She is now house-bound.

Years ago, when Stella's husband Arthur died after a long illness, her married daughter suggested that Stella come and live with her and her husband Mike. Stella refused, saying that she didn't want to be a burden to them. Since then, her daughter has also grown older. Mike retired from work and they moved away to a housing development for retired people. Stella sometimes regrets her decision to stay on in her own home. The neighbourhood has changed a great deal since she and Arthur set up home there as a young married couple more than sixty years ago. She watches people come and go in the street, but she knows almost no one. Her grand-daughter visits regularly, but Stella still finds the days go very slowly.

Although she tries to be cheerful, she often feels lonely. She looks back to the old days when, she believes, people were happier and there was more of a community spirit. "We didn't have much, but what we had, we shared." Stella has spent two periods in hospital in recent years. She is afraid of becoming ill again and perhaps losing her home and independence. She dreads having to leave her flat and "be put in a home". This fear makes her suspicious of un-familiar visitors, whom she believes might make "reports" on her. Recently, a youth club leader visited and suggested that two young people from the club might come and visit Stella regularly. She refused, saying that she had nothing to talk about to two teenagers. Afterwards she regretted her refusal. She hopes that the youth worker will get in touch with her again.

CHAPTER 5

BEING A HUNDRED

At an age when
most older men
are content to
stay at home, this
Japanese climber
joined an
expedition on
Mount Fuji.

In many parts of the world the age-group that is growing more rapidly than any other is the tiny group of old men and women who have reached one hundred years of age. The figures from the last four British censuses show how dramatic the growth has been:

1951	**271 people**
1961	**479**
1971	**1240**
1981	**2410**

In 30 years, the number of centenarians increased ninefold. Britain is typical in experiencing this growth in numbers of the very old. Today there are 34 million people over the age of 80 in the world. By the year 2020, there will be over a hundred million. In all, in the next 40 years, the developing world will see an increase of nearly 400 per cent in the numbers of very old people.

Is it likely that, in years to come, the life-span will go on increasing and that the majority of us will live to a hundred years or more? The answer seems to be "no". Medical progress and, even more importantly, changes in public health, such as better housing, drains and nutrition, have led to a general increase in expectation of life. But there is no evidence of a significant increase in the human life-span.

A biological elite

Centenarians – people who live to be a hundred – are very special people. They are often described as a biological elite. They are the people who have survived the illnesses of childhood, who have avoided heart attacks, strokes and cancers which killed so many of the men and women of their age. Why? One of the important indicators for a long life seems to be heredity. If you have long-lived relatives on both sides of your family, you are more likely to live a long time yourself. Temperament and personality also seem to be involved. A contented, busy life-style and a confidence about your place in a family and a wider social group also help. This positive mental attitude shows in the way many very old people decide to live until a next birthday. It has been suggested that the year 1999 is likely to be one of low mortality because many people will be determined to live on into the

Pablo Picasso was an example of the "biological elite" – individuals who retain their capacities and talents to a great age.

new millennium.

The Valley of the Aged

In some areas of the world it is quite usual to live to be very old and centenarians are fairly common. One of these places is Vilcabamba, in South-west Ecuador in Latin America. This area has been known for many years as the Valley of the Aged. The people are well-known for their great age. One farmer, still working on his land at the age of 104, complained that his plot was six kilometres from his home.

> **"I would really like a plot of land nearer to my home. It's a problem to walk there and back each day."**

Specialists in longevity have studied the population of Vilcabamba and suggest some reasons for its special situation: the altitude is between 4,500 and 5,000 feet above sea level; the climate is almost on the equator, so the difference between the coldest night and the warmest day is only about 10° C. The isolation is another reason: the valley is surrounded by high mountains and its fresh air is free from pollution. The water supply is very high in minerals and people eat mostly vegetables and fruit with only a very little white meat on rare occasions. Medicinal herbs – every family has a knowledge of about a hundred healing plants and roots that grow in the valley – are used to treat illness. Experts may know as many as 300 different herbs. But there are signs of change in Vilcabamba. Where, in the past, people lived from day to day, eating just what their bodies needed and getting supplementary vitamins from the water, they now eat pre-packed and processed food. A new road has been opened, linking the valley to the nearest town and a visitor commented sadly:

"There are now six times as many cases of heart disease as there were when the road opened nine years ago."

Evidence from other societies

In the two other areas of the world where longevity is common, the way of life of the people seems to be remarkably similar to that of the Vilcabambans. The Hunza are high valleys near the China and Afghanistan borders. Here there are large numbers of very old people still living an active working life and, like those in Vilcabamba, eating a mainly vegetable diet.

In the Soviet Union, there is also evidence of a community with a great many centenarians living in a mountain region – in the foothills of the Caucasus Mountains. The 1971 census for the region counted nearly 5,000 people over 100. Again the people in this area consume only about 1,800 calories a day and eat similar foods. They live in farming communities and go on working all their lives, walking long distances every day on rough mountain tracks.

In all the areas where people live to unusual ages there is a common situation. The old people are highly regarded. They live with their families and have a central and privileged position in the group.

There is no forced retirement age and the old people continue to be useful. They continue to perform duties such as weeding in the fields, looking after chickens or other animals, cleaning the house and caring for young children. They are looked up to for their wisdom and their word in the family group is generally law. The old people said that it was important to be independent, and stressed the need to maintain a calm state of mind, free from emotional strains.

This couple can look back on 70 years of happy marriage. They still help and advise their younger relatives.

Adjusting to change

In the past life did not change so much between the generations. However, men and women born in the last decade of the nineteenth century have seen amazing changes. When they were children transport consisted of horse-drawn carts, with only the railway or ships to carry people long distances or to other countries. Now, they see their grand-children happily flying off on holidays abroad and thinking nothing of driving hundreds of miles on a weekend visit.

A man born in 1890 was twenty-four when World War I began. If he survived the dreadful casualty lists, he set up home and raised a family during the Depression. He was 49, already middle-aged, when the World War II began. He probably retired from work around 1955 and has been classed as "an old man" since the early Sixties. He has seen his children grow old, perhaps die, while the world has changed around him. Ordinary working people have a prosperity their parents never dreamed of. Their homes have televisions, fridges, videos, telephones and radios, all invented in their lifetimes.

Very old people have something to teach us all, about adapting graciously to changed situations and changed human relationships. Mrs Dorothy Moriarty will be 100 years old in a few months. She wrote :

> **"And now I have ended up in a wonderful home for the aged. Here I am learning a new way of life, new values, new interests; making friends while keeping up with those I have left behind. And every morning I tell myself 'One day at a time'. Then I look around my cosy room, and I add: 'Count your blessings, Honey'."**

CHAPTER 6

WHAT SORT OF OLD AGE WILL YOU HAVE?

Old people do not always want the company of other older people. Like any other age-group, they enjoy the company of people of different ages and personalities.

At a recent meeting of European family organisations, one of the speakers said, "We have more coffins than cradles". He was illustrating a situation which is widespread in Europe. People are having smaller families at the same time as more people survive to old age.

Governments are already worried about the cost of providing pensions and health and social care for these increasing numbers of retired people, as the number of adults in work declines. What is likely to be the situation in about 50 years time when you're due to retire from work?

Wasted talent

One thing that does seem likely is that we will no longer be able to waste the skills and talents of retired people as we do today. At present, in the developed world, it is only an active and determined minority of elderly people who find new occupations to bring them back into the mainstream of the community, or who are able to carry on their existing occupations into old age. Many others make a largely unrecognised contribution to the lives of families and neighbourhoods, but very little is done, at present, to encourage older people to be actively involved in their local communities. As the balance of the population changes and more and more people retire early from paid work, this situation must change.

Financial security

There are worrying signs that old age may continue, for some people at least, to be a time of poverty, anxiety and a reduced and limited lifestyle. We are already seeing, in the richer countries of the world, deep divisions appearing between rich and poor in the elderly population.

Marketing executives write about the "Grey Market" and about WOOPIES (Well Off Older People). Active, affluent, newly-retired people have been identified as consumers well-worth pursuing. They have money to spend on foreign holidays, cars, expensive items such as caravans or boats, as well as a host of household and garden equipment. They own their own homes and no longer have responsibilities to growing children.

Only a minority of older people live comfortable, affluent lives and can afford to pay for help when they retire.

But a substantial minority of the elderly population are excluded from this rosy picture. In

Britain, for example, pensioners who have only the basic state retirement pension are substantially worse off than the majority of the population.

Recent changes in pensions legislation in Europe suggest that the division between rich and poor retired people may continue. It is likely that the poorest old people will continue to be women. Women who are now old have not built up good pensions during their working lives. Child rearing, caring for elderly relatives and the fact that women's work has generally been less well paid have meant that women entered retirement worse off than men and often dependent on their husbands' pensions.

> **"I manage, but it's a struggle. Prices keep on going up and my money just doesn't keep pace." Mrs Parker, aged 74**

Unfortunately, there is little evidence that this will change. Women still work in the lower paid sectors of employment and they still have careers interrupted by family responsibilities. Divorce is also an important new factor. Women who bring up their children alone or who become divorced in mid-life when their children are grown may face greater insecurity in later life.

A challenge and an opportunity

Governments cannot afford to ignore the demographic changes taking place all over the world. Our ageing societies present us with a situation unknown in human history.

We need to plan now for our own old age. Many

companies provide pre-retirement courses and counselling for employees who are about to retire. But in most cases, this is too little and too late. If we are to become less ageist in our attitudes to old age and in the way we treat older people, then preparation for later life must come earlier.

Better communication between old and young

In developed countries, it is not uncommon for children to grow up without any contact with the older generations. Grandparents and great-grandparents may live far away and divorce splits many families, cutting the grandparent generation off from the children. If older people are to be able to contribute to the lives of the young, we must develop new ways of bringing them together across generation barriers. In the United States and in Europe, many such new ideas are being tried out. A programme called Magic Me began in New York, bringing young children into the nursing homes and hospitals to work with the old residents. Similar projects are run in many European countries, where older people come regularly into schools, to share lessons and learn together. Local history projects are particularly popular, in which the children interview the old people about changes they have seen in their lifetime.

A final word

The ageing population is bringing about profound changes in the structures of our families and communities. The challenge is to treat the changes as an opportunity and not as a problem.

MORE INFORMATION

Further information about ageing and old people can be obtained from

**The Information Department
Help the Aged**
*St James' Walk
London EC1R OBE*

Runs an advice service for old people and their families.

Age Concern England
*60 Pitcairn Road
Mitcham Surrey CR4 3LL*

There are a network of local Age Concern groups all over Britain.

Two specialist organisations dealing with particular problems of old age are

The Alzheimer's Disease Society
*158-160 Balham High Road
London SW12 9BN*

Aims to support the families of patients with information and companionship. Promotes research into the disease.

Carers National Association
*29 Chilworth Mews
London W2 3RG*

Links carers through local groups and compaigns to get more support for relatives caring at home.

Some helpful books to read are

Look Me in the Eye: Old Women, Ageing and Ageism *by Barbara Macdonald and Cynthia Rich, The Women's Press, 1983*

Ageing for Beginners *by Mary Stott Basil, Blackwell, 1981*

WHAT THE WORDS MEAN

ageism discrimination against an individual on grounds of age

arthritis painful disease of the joints

bereavement the experience of losing someone close to you who has died

centenarian a person who is a hundred years old

chronic disease an illness which continues for a long time, like arthritis – the opposite of acute disease, an illness like chicken pox

dementia mental condition caused by brain failure because of the abnormal death of brain cells

demography the study of statistics concerning human population e.g. births, deaths, diseases

dependency the condition of being in need of help and support from another person

euthanasia deliberately allowing or causing the painless death of someone for compassionate reasons

extended family a household in which three or more generations live together

geriatric medical term meaning 'concerning old age', as in geriatric medicine

gerontology the study of human ageing

heredity the process by which children inherit the nature and characteristics of parents or other ancestors

life-expectancy the average length of time a human being of a particular age may expect to live

life-span the length of time between birth and death in a human being

migration a permanent move to a different area, as in a move from country to city, or to a different country

occupational pension a pension paid wholly or in part by an individual's employer

Photographic Credits:
Cover: Zefa; pages 4, 33, 34, 46, 49 and 52: Frank Spooner Agency; pages 6 and 13: Robert Harding Library; pages 9, 11, 14, 18, 24, 37 and 40: Network Photographers; pages 20, 21, 29, 30, 42, 43, 54 and 57: Magnum Photos.